Lesbian Queries?

By
Jennifer Hertz
and
Martha Ertman

The Naiad Press, Inc.
1990

Printed in the United States of America
First Edition

Cover design by Pat Tong and Bonnie Liss
    (Phoenix Graphics)
Typeset by Sandi Stancil

Library of Congress Cataloging-in-Publication Data

Hertz, Jennifer, 1964–
    Lesbian queries : the book of lesbian questions / by Jennifer
Hertz and Martha Ertman.
        p.   cm.
    ISBN 0-941483-67-3
    1. Lesbianism--Miscellanea.   I. Ertman, Martha, 1963–
II. Title.
HQ75.5.H46   1990
306.76′63--dc20   89-48961
                                                                    CIP

*To the girls who inspired the questions
and the women who will answer them.*

ABOUT THE AUTHORS

Martha Ertman

Martha Ertman mostly thinks about politics but is trying to develop the aesthetic side of her life. She recently finished studying law in Chicago and does not yet regret it. Though she received her Wellesley B.A. in Psycho-Biology, her ideal job is a T.V. talk show host, where she hopes to use more of the psych than the biology.

Jennifer Hertz

Jennifer Hertz currently plays rugby and studies law in Chicago. While her passion is mathematics, she is content being a loosehead prop who will someday work in the field of lesbian legal defense. She is thrilled that her longtime friendship with Martha Ertman has finally resulted in a marketable product.

ACKNOWLEDGMENTS

We would like to thank our friends and ex-lovers for patiently listening to these queries, laughing with us and at us. In particular, Alisa R. Surkis, Jane Jarcho, Anna Holzhauer, Karen A. Simonsen, Tracy Walton, Kim Johns, Stephanie Gaynor, Jill Bogosian, Nancy Robie, Amy Nutt, Dave Biggs, Sam Corsak, Stephanie Dorgan Walton, and the whole Boston Women's Rugby Club.

ACKNOWLEDGMENTS

Lesbian Queries

?

By
**Jennifer
Hertz**
and
**Martha
Ertman**

1

Is it possible to maintain a healthy gay identity if the majority of your friends are straight? What do you consider a healthy gay identity?

2

What's your working definition for "lesbian?"

3

Is meeting your date's cats as stressful as meeting her children? How about her parents?

4

Do lesbians have a more positive body image than straight women? Is this due to feminism?

5

Is it politically problematic to have subscriptions to both *On Our Backs* and *Off Our Backs*?

6

Are you more butch or more femme?

7

Is fisting hard-core or mainstream? Are you hard-core or mainstream?

8

Which is worse, butch on butch or femme on femme?

9

If there were no social stigma attached to it, and it was 100% safe, would you sleep with a prostitute?

10

How many people is too many to have slept with before you are twenty? Thirty? Forty? Fifty? Sixty? A lifetime?

11

How long would you have to date before you would consider a lifetime relationship with a partner? When your friends enter into "lifetime" unions, do you believe them? When you enter into a "lifetime" union, do you believe you?

12

What do you think of threesomes? Have you ever been in a threesome? If you get into a threesome, what should be the relationships among the players?? A couple plus one? Three randoms? Three friends?

13

When did you first do *It* with a woman? What did you do? What constitutes *It*?

14

If you were a perfect bisexual, 50/50 exactly, would you choose to lead a gay lifestyle, a straight one, or a bisexual one?

15

If you had to choose one role for the rest of your life would you be a top or a bottom? If you had to choose one partner for the rest of your life, would you choose a top or a bottom?

16

Would you date yourself? Would you get serious with yourself

17

Name the two most dangerous emotions.

18

How do you feel about boy children at the music festivals? Under 5? Under 10? Under 21?

19

What's your best line used to determine whether or not a person is a lesbian?

20

Would you rather be better in bed than your lover or have her be better in bed than you?

21

Are you a jumper or a jumpee? Are you a dumper or a dumpee? Do you think there's a system of justice whereby if you dump someone, the next person will dump you?

22

How many fingers do you use to penetrate your lover? What is your dominant finger?

23

Do you make love to a new lover the way you like to be made love to or the way your last lover liked you to make love to her?

24

Would it be worse to be left for a man or a woman?

25

Are you a cat person or a dog person?

26

Where's the most public place you've had sex?

27

Would you rather your ex-lover's new lover be ugly or attractive? Intelligent or stupid? Would it matter if she had dumped you or you had dumped her?

28

What is the longest time you've been with a lover and not sexually active with that lover? How long would you remain involved in a non-sexual relationship?

29

What is the longest span of time you've gone without
sex since you began to be sexually active?

30

Have you ever cheated on a lover?

31

Do you believe in non-monogamy? Do you believe in monogamy?

32

Do you prefer the phrase sexual preference, sexual orientation, or affectional preference? Are there others you use?

33

If you visited your parents' home with a lover, would you stay in the same bed? Would you have sex in your parents' home?

34

How frequently do you get mistaken for a man? How do you respond? How frequently do you get mistaken for a het? How do you respond?

35

Have you (or anyone else) found your G-spot?

36

Would you become involved with someone you knew to be in a committed, supposedly monogamous relationship? How about for just one night?

37

Are you friends with your ex-lovers?

38

Would you rather watch sports or play them?

39

Can you remember the first lesbian you met? Did she scare you?

40

Have you (or would you) make a pass at a straight woman? A boss? A professor?

41

Do you have bumper stickers on your car? What do they say? Can you tell a dyke from the bumper stickers on her car?

42

Are you in psychotherapy? Can you name six lesbians who are not, never were, and probably never will be in psychotherapy?

43

Do you have sex while menstruating? Oral sex? Digital?

44

The women's music festival is on the same day as the senior prom. Which do you go to?

45

Would you (or have you) included a lover in a will? Do you have legal arrangements which name your lover as next of kin?

46

Your Republican brother is getting married and does not invite your lover to the ceremony. Do you attend? Do you bring your lover? Do you send a gift?

47

Does it make sense to have a category called lesbians who fuck men?

48

Your corporation is having a must attend social function. Everyone is bringing their significant others. Do you bring yours?

49

If you were treated unjustly at a job based on sexual preference, would you take legal action? Have you?

50

Do you bring your lover to parent-teacher conferences? PTA meetings?

51

Your mother finds The Coming Out Stories under your mattress. How do you explain?

52

A homophobic cousin makes a gay joke at Thanksgiving. How do you respond? What if it's a co-worker at a staff meeting?

53

If you were a man, would you be gay, straight or bisexual?

54

Do you have any gay siblings? Are one or more of your parents gay? Do you have any straight siblings?

55

If you have (or will have) children, would you rather they be gay or straight? Boys or girls?

56

What turns you on more, reading an erotic story or watching an erotic movie?

57

Can you name everyone you've slept with, first and last names? Would you?

58

Given the choice, would you pick the family you have? If not, who would you choose?

59

If your lover hit you, would you walk? Have you ever been struck by a lover? How do you think the incidence of battering in the lesbian community compares to the incidence of battering in the straight community?

60

What percentage of lesbians do you think have orgasms? What percentage of the time they have sex?

61

Would you shave your head for $100? $1,000? $10,000? How about your legs?

62

Would you agree to have your non-dominant hand cut off (amputated) if it meant the end of oppression of women? Gays?

63

Would you be a man for a week? A month? A year? Longer?

64

Are feminism and affluence mutually exclusive?

65

Would your parents like your lover more if she were a man?

66

How do you define bisexuality? Are bisexual pride and gay pride compatible? Would you date a bisexual?

67

Are blondes underrepresented in the lesbian community? Why?

68

When did you first come out to yourself? When did you first come out to another person?

69

If you had to choose between coming out and losing your parents and/or siblings, would you? Did you?

70

How long were you out before you could say the word gay? Lesbian? Dyke? What do you call yourself now?

71

Is there any decent term to describe female genitalia? Is cunt or pussy more palatable than vagina?

72

What terms for female genitalia do you use in bed? On the street? In the classroom? To your parents? To your children?

73

What happened to the people you used to be afraid of? (Particularly those short-haired tough dykes you met when you first came out.)

74

How do you spell woman/womyn/womon/wimmin? Has
your choice changed over the years? Do you think
spelling is important?

75

Who is the oldest person you've come out to? The
youngest?

76

Of the people you've slept with, how many of your "first times," were you drunk?

77

If you had a one night stand with a stranger, would you use her toothbrush? Would you let her use yours?

78

If you slept with a man for the hell of it, would you tell your best friend? Housemates or roommate(s)? Siblings? Co-workers? Lover?

79

What occupation, profession, or trade has the greatest percentage of lesbians? Are there more lesbian massage therapists than lesbian lawyers or professors? Are there any lesbian talk show hosts? Don't you wish there were?

80

Of the people you've slept with, for how many has it been their first time?

81

If you were a domesticated cat would you want your owner to give you only vegetarian food?

82

Why do lesbians like cats so much?

83

If you could make a movie or write a book about one of your relationships, would you choose your most torrid romance? Most stable? Longest lasting?

84

Is it possible or desirable to get over the hatred of men? Your parents? Ex-lovers?

85

All other things being equal, is it worse to get dumped for a woman or a man?

86

What exactly are those brown specks in wild rice?

87

Does tapioca pudding qualify as vegetarian food? Mincemeat pie? Fruitcake?

88

Is it possible to be radical and still be rational?

89

If a lesbian candidate for president espoused politics entirely different from your own, would you vote for her?

90

If you could eliminate all men (non-violently if your politics require) by dropping this book on the ground, would you?

91

If you could, would you live your life at the Michigan Womyn's Music Festival? What if they made heat and hot water available? Plumbing? Modern housing? Would it still be Michigan?

92

How many times can a person fall in love in her lifetime?

93

Would you have a baby by egg fusion with your current lover? Ex-lover? Any lover? How would you decide who carries the baby?

94

Is lesbianism defined by sleeping with girls? Can you be a lesbian without sleeping with girls?

95

Do S&M writers or lesbian pornographers lead lives as wild as those portrayed in their stories? Do they base their work on life experiences?

96

Would you sleep with a woman for money? Does it matter whether she's straight, bisexual, or gay? Would you sleep with a man for money? Would his sexuality change your answer?

97

You're as hungry, sleepy, and horny as you've ever been; in what order do you satisfy these needs? Your favorite food, bed, and source of nookie are immediately available.

98

Is there still a gay/straight split in the feminist movement?

99

Is true equality possible, or is one person always dominant in a relationship (socially, not necessarily sexually)? Is true equality characterized by switching dominant and subservient roles?

100

How do you define S&M? Which behaviors qualify and which do not?

101

Could you trust a lover who left someone else to be with you?

102

Can long distance relationships work?

103

What qualifies as a dykey car? Why? Do you buy American cars or foreign cars?

104

What sport is most played by lesbians? What women's sport is predominantly straight? Why?

105

Is there more alcoholism in the lesbian community than in the general population? How about compared to gay men?

106

Are lesbians less or more discriminated against than gay men? Is it equal?

107

Do you have a "type?" What is it? Would you date her? Get involved? Be friends?

108

Is there such a thing as politically correct or feminist sex? If so, what is it?

109

How many times do you come out in an average day? Is it getting easier as you've been out longer? How far along in the coming out process are you? What's the next step?

110

Is there some political problem about scoping straight women with a straight man? Is there any value in making them comfortable with lesbians in this way? Is there any value in any contact with straight men?

111

Do you remember the first time you went to a gay bar? With whom did you go? Were you out to yourself or others at the time? What was your initial response?

112

Who is the lesbian you admire most and why?

113

Do you generally feel superior, inferior, or equal to your lovers?

114

Is how "out" you are a function of personality, politics, occupation or something else? Is it class related? Race? Gender?

115

Have you ever gotten someone drunk to get her to sleep with you?

116

Do you feel that it's important for your children to play with kids of straight couples? Lesbian and/or gay couples?

117

Do you have more intense orgasms masturbating or having sex with another person? How about using electrical aids?

118

Why don't your leg and armpit hair grow as long as your head hair? What about your eyebrows?

119

Have you ever gone to a bar with a toothbrush and spare t-shirt in your bag (or car)?

120

Would you date a man just to meet his sister?

121

Do you prefer sex in the a.m. or p.m.? Any particular day?

122

Would you go to a male gynecologist? Do you think it's important to tell your doctor, midwife, or nurse practitioner that you're gay?

123

What's your idea of a perfect Saturday? What's your lover's idea of a perfect Saturday? Is it important that these are similar?

124

What's the best city for lesbians in the United States? Outside the United States?

125

What are two things that you just know about yourself without any need for reinforcement?

126

What's your best purchase under $5? $10? $20?

127

What are the meaningful distinctions between erotica and pornography?

128

Can a business stay in the black with a policy of sliding scale fees? What are the pros and cons of consensus oriented management?

129

Is your house or apartment wheelchair accessible?

130

Name two non-sexual uses for K-Y jelly.

131

Would you buy or use a butt plug?

132

Would you perform a strip tease for your lover? A one night stand? A casual date?

133

Why are there so many more men's bars than women's bars?

134

How can lesbians reconcile demanding that gay men fight for our issues and still maintain women-only spaces?

135

You can pick a lesbian for the next U.S. president — who is she?

136

What's your working definition of feminism and feminist? Is there such a thing as post-feminism?

137

Is hierarchy always a bad (i.e., patriarchal, sexist, etc.) thing?

138

What's the biggest evil in the world, or what's the most powerful and destructive "ism?" Examples are sexism, racism, homophobia, classism, ablism, etc.

139

If your boss was a lesbian, would you sleep with her just to get ahead?

140

What's the ideal number of times per week to have sex — assuming no other problems in your relationship and an involvement of longer than six months?

141

What percentage of long term (over 2 years) lesbian relationships suffer from bed death?

142

Do your lover's cats side with your lover in an argument? How do you feel about this?

143

Is it antifeminist to bleach your mustache?

144

Would you avoid dating a poet? musician? or author? for fear of public humiliation?

145

If you thought the lesbian/feminist revolution was going to happen in your lifetime, would you disrupt your life to work for it?

146

What do you do if you like your lover's mother more than your lover? Your mother's lover?

147

Would you pose nude for a local magazine? National? Gay? Lesbian? Straight? Political? Pornographic?

148

Do gay men and lesbians have anything in common other than same-sex partners?

149

Are there out lesbians represented in the mainstream media? Who are they? If you cannot name more than two, why can't you?

150

Can sex be better under the influence of drugs?

151

Have you ever dated a woman less than half your age or more than twice your age?

152

If you could be any race, what race would you be? Nationality? Gender? Species?

153

What are the first three things you would do as the $10 million winner in the American Family Sweepstakes? Is it politically incorrect to accept money from a group called American Family?

154

Are you a man-hater? A separatist? What are the differences between these categories?

155

Are you capable of killing an ex-lover? Would you actively plot for an ex-lover's demise? Are you capable of killing an assailant? Are your answers to these questions related?

156

Are you capable of killing men, at random?

157

Why are gay men generally more attentive to dress and appearance than lesbians?

158

Are lesbians overrepresented at women's colleges?

159

Is your lesbianism a choice or were you born that way? Do you think the same answer applies to most lesbians? How about gay men?

160

Is it true that workable relationships require one woman to be a butch and the other to be a femme? Do you see these patterns in gay men's relationships?

161

Are more lesbians in psychotherapy than straight women?

162

What's your favorite stereotype of lesbians? Least favorite?

163

Who is the most supportive straight person in your life? What does she or he do that make her or him so supportive?

164

What's the funniest/most ignorant question anyone's ever asked you about being a lesbian?

165

Why is there such a split between political and bar lesbians? Is the split related to class? Race? Education?

166

What's for dinner?

167

How would you respond if the woman you're casually dating tells you she's crazy?

168

If you are allowed to save one man in the lesbian/feminist revolution, who would you save?

169

Are men intrinsically violent? Are women intrinsically non-violent? If not, why haven't we risen in armed revolution in the past 3,000 years?

170

Are there more politically conservative lesbians now than there were 20 years ago? How do you feel about Gay Republicans?

171

Would you rather be Gertrude Stein or Alice B. Toklas?

172

Can you name three stereotypes of lesbians or gays in general which are accurate? Inaccurate?

173

How has the definition of politically correct changed since the early 80s? What would we have considered PC in the 30s, 40s, 50s, 60s, 70s?

174

Why are lesbians (by reputation anyway) more likely to sleep with relatively few people while gay men seem to sleep with so many people?

175

Is lesbianism a magnification of femininity? Male homosexuality a magnification of masculinity?

176

What is the connection between lesbianism and athletics? i.e., why is it that so many jocks are dykes and dykes are jocks?

177

Name five sources of non-meat protein.

178

What adjective or adjectives were most frequently ascribed to you as a child?

179

What's your favorite lesbian themed movie? What's your favorite lesbian themed book?

180

If you don't smoke, what brand of cigarettes would you smoke if you did smoke?

181

What lesbian and/or gay event would you not be caught dead missing?

182

Can the world accurately be divided into people who seek intimacy and those who see intimacy and run in the other direction?

183

Are jocks generally butch? By the same token are dyke socialites generally femme?

184

Is there such a thing as dyke chic? What does it look like?

185

What's your opinion of the gay political agenda of dragging closeted politicians out of the closet? Does it matter whether they are pursuing pro-gay or anti-gay agendas?

186

What's your ideal job? Would you rather work for a man or a woman? A large corporation or a small group that operates on consensus?

187

Should transvestites be barred from women-only space? How about transsexuals? If so, how would you enforce either rule?

188

Do you understand all the abbreviations in the personal ads?

189

Have you ever answered a personal ad? Put one in? Were you happy with the respondents?

190

Why do gay men often call themselves and each other "girl" and "she?" Do you call your dyke friends "boy" and "he?" Why or why not?

191

What do your parents (or children) say when asked by straight friends or co-workers whether you have a boyfriend/husband? What would you have them say?

192

If you could remake a classic romantic movie with two women in the lead roles, which movie would you choose? Who would you cast as the leading ladies? What plot twists, if any, would you add?

193

Does the idea of a "zipless fuck" appeal to you? Do you think it appeals to many lesbians? Gay men? Straight men or women?

194

Would you formally exchange vows? In a church or temple? If your own church or temple refused, would you approach other churches or temples? Would you exchange vows before a rabbi, minister, or priest? Would you invite your parents? Siblings? Cousins? Co-workers? Would you go on a honeymoon to a resort in the Poconos? Inner Mongolia?

195

How old were you when you had your first crush on a woman?

196

Do straight boys really kiss gross or do we just think so because we're lesbians?

197

When you meet a woman named Jennifer Janedaughter, do you wonder what her name used to be?

A few of the publications of
THE NAIAD PRESS, INC.
P.O. Box 10543 ● Tallahassee, Florida 32302
Phone (904) 539-5965
Mail orders welcome. Please include 15% postage.

CLUB 12 by Amanda Kyle Williams. 288 pp. Espionage thriller
featuring a lesbian agent!　　　　　ISBN 0-941483-64-9　　$8.95

LESBIAN QUERIES by Hertz & Ertman. 112 pp. The questions
you were too embarrassed to ask.　　ISBN 0-941483-67-3　　8.95

THEME FOR DIVERSE INSTRUMENTS by Jane Rule.
208 pp. Powerful romantic lesbian stories.　ISBN 0-941483-63-0　8.95

PRIORITIES by Lynda Lyons 288 pp. Science fiction with a
twist.　　　　　　　　　　　　　ISBN 0-941483-66-5　　8.95

DEATH DOWN UNDER by Claire McNab. 240 pp. 3rd Det.
Insp. Carol Ashton mystery.　　　ISBN 0-941483-39-8　　8.95

MONTANA FEATHERS by Penny Hayes. 256 pp. Vivian and
Elizabeth find love in frontier Montana.　ISBN 0-941483-61-4　8.95

CHESAPEAKE PROJECT by Phyllis Horn. 304 pp. Jessie &
Meredith in perilous adventure.　　ISBN 0-941483-58-4　　8.95

LIFESTYLES by Jackie Calhoun. 224 pp. Contemporary Lesbian
lives and loves.　　　　　　　　ISBN 0-941483-57-6　　8.95

VIRAGO by Karen Marie Christa Minns. 208 pp. Darsen has
chosen Ginny.　　　　　　　　　ISBN 0-941483-56-8　　8.95

WILDERNESS TREK by Dorothy Tell. 192 pp. Six women on
vacation learning "new" skills.　　ISBN 0-941483-60-6　　8.95

MURDER BY THE BOOK by Pat Welch. 256 pp. A Helen
Black Mystery. First in a series.　　ISBN 0-941483-59-2　　8.95

BERRIGAN by Vicki P. McConnell. 176 pp. Youthful Lesbian–
romantic, idealistic Berrigan.　　　ISBN 0-941483-55-X　　8.95

LESBIANS IN GERMANY by Lillian Faderman & B. Eriksson.
128 pp. Fiction, poetry, essays.　　ISBN 0-941483-62-2　　8.95

THE BEVERLY MALIBU by Katherine V. Forrest. 288 pp. A
Kate Delafield Mystery. 3rd in a series.　ISBN 0-941483-47-9　16.95

THERE'S SOMETHING I'VE BEEN MEANING TO TELL
YOU Ed. by Loralee MacPike. 288 pp. Gay men and lesbians
coming out to their children.　　　ISBN 0-941483-44-4　　9.95
　　　　　　　　　　　　　　　ISBN 0-941483-54-1　16.95

LIFTING BELLY by Gertrude Stein. Ed. by Rebecca Mark. 104
pp. Erotic poetry.　　　　　　　ISBN 0-941483-51-7　　8.95
　　　　　　　　　　　　　　　ISBN 0-941483-53-3　14.95

ROSE PENSKI by Roz Perry. 192 pp. Adult lovers in a long-term
relationship.　　　　　　　　　ISBN 0-941483-37-1　　8.95

AFTER THE FIRE by Jane Rule. 256 pp. Warm, human novel
by this incomparable author.   ISBN 0-941483-45-2   8.95
SUE SLATE, PRIVATE EYE by Lee Lynch. 176 pp. The gay
folk of Peacock Alley are *all* cats.   ISBN 0-941483-52-5   8.95
CHRIS by Randy Salem. 224 pp. Golden oldie. Handsome Chris
and her adventures.   ISBN 0-941483-42-8   8.95
THREE WOMEN by March Hastings. 232 pp. Golden oldie. A
triangle among wealthy sophisticates.   ISBN 0-941483-43-6   8.95
RICE AND BEANS by Valeria Taylor. 232 pp. Love and
romance on poverty row.   ISBN 0-941483-41-X   8.95
PLEASURES by Robbi Sommers. 204 pp. Unprecedented
eroticism.   ISBN 0-941483-49-5   8.95
EDGEWISE by Camarin Grae. 372 pp. Spellbinding
adventure.   ISBN 0-941483-19-3   9.95
FATAL REUNION by Claire McNab. 216 pp. 2nd Det. Inspec.
Carol Ashton mystery.   ISBN 0-941483-40-1   8.95
KEEP TO ME STRANGER by Sarah Aldridge. 372 pp. Romance
set in a department store dynasty.   ISBN 0-941483-38-X   9.95
HEARTSCAPE by Sue Gambill. 204 pp. American lesbian in
Portugal.   ISBN 0-941483-33-9   8.95
IN THE BLOOD by Lauren Wright Douglas. 252 pp. Lesbian
science fiction adventure fantasy   ISBN 0-941483-22-3   8.95
THE BEE'S KISS by Shirley Verel. 216 pp. Delicate, delicious
romance.   ISBN 0-941483-36-3   8.95
RAGING MOTHER MOUNTAIN by Pat Emmerson. 264 pp.
Furosa Firechild's adventures in Wonderland. ISBN 0-941483-35-5 8.95
IN EVERY PORT by Karin Kallmaker. 228 pp. Jessica's sexy,
adventuresome travels.   ISBN 0-941483-37-7   8.95
OF LOVE AND GLORY by Evelyn Kennedy. 192 pp. Exciting
WWII romance.   ISBN 0-941483-32-0   8.95
CLICKING STONES by Nancy Tyler Glenn. 288 pp. Love
transcending time.   ISBN 0-941483-31-2   8.95
SURVIVING SISTERS by Gail Pass. 252 pp. Powerful love
story.   ISBN 0-941483-16-9   8.95
SOUTH OF THE LINE by Catherine Ennis. 216 pp. Civil War
adventure.   ISBN 0-941483-29-0   8.95
WOMAN PLUS WOMAN by Dolores Klaich. 300 pp. Supurb
Lesbian overview.   ISBN 0-941483-28-2   9.95
SLOW DANCING AT MISS POLLY'S by Sheila Ortiz Taylor.
96 pp. Lesbian Poetry   ISBN 0-941483-30-4   7.95
DOUBLE DAUGHTER by Vicki P. McConnell. 216 pp. A Nyla
Wade Mystery, third in the series.   ISBN 0-941483-26-6   8.95

HEAVY GILT by Delores Klaich. 192 pp. Lesbian detective/
disappearing homophobes/upper class gay society.
       ISBN 0-941483-25-8 8.95

THE FINER GRAIN by Denise Ohio. 216 pp. Brilliant young
college lesbian novel.   ISBN 0-941483-11-8 8.95

THE AMAZON TRAIL by Lee Lynch. 216 pp. Life, travel & lore
of famous lesbian author.   ISBN 0-941483-27-4 8.95

HIGH CONTRAST by Jessie Lattimore. 264 pp. Women of the
Crystal Palace.   ISBN 0-941483-17-7 8.95

OCTOBER OBSESSION by Meredith More. Josie's rich, secret
Lesbian life.   ISBN 0-941483-18-5 8.95

LESBIAN CROSSROADS by Ruth Baetz. 276 pp. Contemporary
Lesbian lives.   ISBN 0-941483-21-5 9.95

BEFORE STONEWALL: THE MAKING OF A GAY AND
LESBIAN COMMUNITY by Andrea Weiss & Greta Schiller.
96 pp., 25 illus.   ISBN 0-941483-20-7 7.95

WE WALK THE BACK OF THE TIGER by Patricia A. Murphy.
192 pp. Romantic Lesbian novel/beginning women's movement.
       ISBN 0-941483-13-4 8.95

SUNDAY'S CHILD by Joyce Bright. 216 pp. Lesbian athletics, at
last the novel about sports. ISBN 0-941483-12-6 8.95

OSTEN'S BAY by Zenobia N. Vole. 204 pp. Sizzling adventure
romance set on Bonaire.   ISBN 0-941483-15-0 8.95

LESSONS IN MURDER by Claire McNab. 216 pp. 1st Det. Inspec.
Carol Ashton mystery — erotic tension!. ISBN 0-941483-14-2 8.95

YELLOWTHROAT by Penny Hayes. 240 pp. Margarita, bandit,
kidnaps Julia.   ISBN 0-941483-10-X 8.95

SAPPHISTRY: THE BOOK OF LESBIAN SEXUALITY by
Pat Califia. 3d edition, revised. 208 pp. ISBN 0-941483-24-X 8.95

CHERISHED LOVE by Evelyn Kennedy. 192 pp. Erotic
Lesbian love story.   ISBN 0-941483-08-8 8.95

LAST SEPTEMBER by Helen R. Hull. 208 pp. Six stories & a
glorious novella.   ISBN 0-941483-09-6 8.95

THE SECRET IN THE BIRD by Camarin Grae. 312 pp. Striking,
psychological suspense novel. ISBN 0-941483-05-3 8.95

TO THE LIGHTNING by Catherine Ennis. 208 pp. Romantic
Lesbian 'Robinson Crusoe' adventure. ISBN 0-941483-06-1 8.95

THE OTHER SIDE OF VENUS by Shirley Verel. 224 pp.
Luminous, romantic love story. ISBN 0-941483-07-X 8.95

DREAMS AND SWORDS by Katherine V. Forrest. 192 pp.
Romantic, erotic, imaginative stories. ISBN 0-941483-03-7 8.95

MEMORY BOARD by Jane Rule. 336 pp. Memorable novel
about an aging Lesbian couple.   ISBN 0-941483-02-9   9.95

THE ALWAYS ANONYMOUS BEAST by Lauren Wright
Douglas. 224 pp. A Caitlin Reese mystery. First in a series.
                                        ISBN 0-941483-04-5   8.95

SEARCHING FOR SPRING by Patricia A. Murphy. 224 pp.
Novel about the recovery of love.   ISBN 0-941483-00-2   8.95

DUSTY'S QUEEN OF HEARTS DINER by Lee Lynch. 240 pp.
Romantic blue-collar novel.   ISBN 0-941483-01-0   8.95

PARENTS MATTER by Ann Muller. 240 pp. Parents'
relationships with Lesbian daughters and gay sons.
                                        ISBN 0-930044-91-6   9.95

THE PEARLS by Shelley Smith. 176 pp. Passion and fun in
the Caribbean sun.   ISBN 0-930044-93-2   7.95

MAGDALENA by Sarah Aldridge. 352 pp. Epic Lesbian novel
set on three continents.   ISBN 0-930044-99-1   8.95

THE BLACK AND WHITE OF IT by Ann Allen Shockley.
144 pp. Short stories.   ISBN 0-930044-96-7   7.95

SAY JESUS AND COME TO ME by Ann Allen Shockley. 288
pp. Contemporary romance.   ISBN 0-930044-98-3   8.95

LOVING HER by Ann Allen Shockley. 192 pp. Romantic love
story.   ISBN 0-930044-97-5   7.95

MURDER AT THE NIGHTWOOD BAR by Katherine V.
Forrest. 240 pp. A Kate Delafield mystery. Second in a series.
                                        ISBN 0-930044-92-4   8.95

ZOE'S BOOK by Gail Pass. 224 pp. Passionate, obsessive love
story.   ISBN 0-930044-95-9   7.95

WINGED DANCER by Camarin Grae. 228 pp. Erotic Lesbian
adventure story.   ISBN 0-930044-88-6   8.95

PAZ by Camarin Grae. 336 pp. Romantic Lesbian adventurer
with the power to change the world.   ISBN 0-930044-89-4   8.95

SOUL SNATCHER by Camarin Grae. 224 pp. A puzzle, an
adventure, a mystery — Lesbian romance. ISBN 0-930044-90-8   8.95

THE LOVE OF GOOD WOMEN by Isabel Miller. 224 pp.
Long-awaited new novel by the author of the beloved *Patience
and Sarah.*   ISBN 0-930044-81-9   8.95

THE HOUSE AT PELHAM FALLS by Brenda Weathers. 240
pp. Suspenseful Lesbian ghost story.   ISBN 0-930044-79-7   7.95

HOME IN YOUR HANDS by Lee Lynch. 240 pp. More stories
from the author of *Old Dyke Tales.*   ISBN 0-930044-80-0   7.95

EACH HAND A MAP by Anita Skeen. 112 pp. Real-life poems
that touch us all.   ISBN 0-930044-82-7   6.95

SURPLUS by Sylvia Stevenson. 342 pp. A classic early Lesbian
novel.   ISBN 0-930044-78-9   7.95

PEMBROKE PARK by Michelle Martin. 256 pp. Derring-do
and daring romance in Regency England.   ISBN 0-930044-77-0   7.95

THE LONG TRAIL by Penny Hayes. 248 pp. Vivid adventures
of two women in love in the old west.   ISBN 0-930044-76-2   8.95

HORIZON OF THE HEART by Shelley Smith. 192 pp. Hot
romance in summertime New England.   ISBN 0-930044-75-4   7.95

AN EMERGENCE OF GREEN by Katherine V. Forrest. 288
pp. Powerful novel of sexual discovery.   ISBN 0-930044-69-X   8.95

THE LESBIAN PERIODICALS INDEX edited by Claire
Potter. 432 pp. Author & subject index.   ISBN 0-930044-74-6   29.95

DESERT OF THE HEART by Jane Rule. 224 pp. A classic;
basis for the movie Desert Hearts.   ISBN 0-930044-73-8   7.95

SPRING FORWARD/FALL BACK by Sheila Ortiz Taylor.
288 pp. Literary novel of timeless love.   ISBN 0-930044-70-3   7.95

FOR KEEPS by Elisabeth Nonas. 144 pp. Contemporary novel
about losing and finding love.   ISBN 0-930044-71-1   7.95

TORCHLIGHT TO VALHALLA by Gale Wilhelm. 128 pp.
Classic novel by a great Lesbian writer.   ISBN 0-930044-68-1   7.95

LESBIAN NUNS: BREAKING SILENCE edited by Rosemary
Curb and Nancy Manahan. 432 pp. Unprecedented autobiographies
of religious life.   ISBN 0-930044-62-2   9.95

THE SWASHBUCKLER by Lee Lynch. 288 pp. Colorful novel
set in Greenwich Village in the sixties.   ISBN 0-930044-66-5   8.95

MISFORTUNE'S FRIEND by Sarah Aldridge. 320 pp. Historical Lesbian novel set on two continents.   ISBN 0-930044-67-3   7.95

A STUDIO OF ONE'S OWN by Ann Stokes. Edited by
Dolores Klaich. 128 pp. Autobiography.   ISBN 0-930044-64-9   7.95

SEX VARIANT WOMEN IN LITERATURE by Jeannette
Howard Foster. 448 pp. Literary history.   ISBN 0-930044-65-7   8.95

A HOT-EYED MODERATE by Jane Rule. 252 pp. Hard-hitting
essays on gay life; writing; art.   ISBN 0-930044-57-6   7.95

INLAND PASSAGE AND OTHER STORIES by Jane Rule.
288 pp. Wide-ranging new collection.   ISBN 0-930044-56-8   7.95

WE TOO ARE DRIFTING by Gale Wilhelm. 128 pp. Timeless
Lesbian novel, a masterpiece.   ISBN 0-930044-61-4   6.95

AMATEUR CITY by Katherine V. Forrest. 224 pp. A Kate
Delafield mystery. First in a series.   ISBN 0-930044-55-X   8.95

THE SOPHIE HOROWITZ STORY by Sarah Schulman. 176
pp. Engaging novel of madcap intrigue.   ISBN 0-930044-54-1   7.95

THE BURNTON WIDOWS by Vickie P. McConnell. 272 pp. A
Nyla Wade mystery, second in the series.   ISBN 0-930044-52-5   7.95

OLD DYKE TALES by Lee Lynch. 224 pp. Extraordinary
stories of our diverse Lesbian lives.   ISBN 0-930044-51-7   8.95

DAUGHTERS OF A CORAL DAWN by Katherine V. Forrest.
240 pp. Novel set in a Lesbian new world.   ISBN 0-930044-50-9   8.95

THE PRICE OF SALT by Claire Morgan. 288 pp. A milestone
novel, a beloved classic.   ISBN 0-930044-49-5   8.95

AGAINST THE SEASON by Jane Rule. 224 pp. Luminous,
complex novel of interrelationships.   ISBN 0-930044-48-7   8.95

LOVERS IN THE PRESENT AFTERNOON by Kathleen
Fleming. 288 pp. A novel about recovery and growth.
    ISBN 0-930044-46-0   8.95

TOOTHPICK HOUSE by Lee Lynch. 264 pp. Love between
two Lesbians of different classes.   ISBN 0-930044-45-2   7.95

MADAME AURORA by Sarah Aldridge. 256 pp. Historical
novel featuring a charismatic "seer."   ISBN 0-930044-44-4   7.95

CURIOUS WINE by Katherine V. Forrest. 176 pp. Passionate
Lesbian love story, a best-seller.   ISBN 0-930044-43-6   8.95

BLACK LESBIAN IN WHITE AMERICA by Anita Cornwell.
141 pp. Stories, essays, autobiography.   ISBN 0-930044-41-X   7.95

CONTRACT WITH THE WORLD by Jane Rule. 340 pp.
Powerful, panoramic novel of gay life.   ISBN 0-930044-28-2   9.95

MRS. PORTER'S LETTER by Vicki P. McConnell. 224 pp.
The first Nyla Wade mystery.   ISBN 0-930044-29-0   7.95

TO THE CLEVELAND STATION by Carol Anne Douglas.
192 pp. Interracial Lesbian love story.   ISBN 0-930044-27-4   6.95

THE NESTING PLACE by Sarah Aldridge. 224 pp. A
three-woman triangle—love conquers all!   ISBN 0-930044-26-6   7.95

THIS IS NOT FOR YOU by Jane Rule. 284 pp. A letter to a
beloved is also an intricate novel.   ISBN 0-930044-25-8   8.95

FAULTLINE by Sheila Ortiz Taylor. 140 pp. Warm, funny,
literate story of a startling family.   ISBN 0-930044-24-X   6.95

THE LESBIAN IN LITERATURE by Barbara Grier. 3d ed.
Foreword by Maida Tilchen. 240 pp. Comprehensive bibliography.
Literary ratings; rare photos.   ISBN 0-930044-23-1   7.95

ANNA'S COUNTRY by Elizabeth Lang. 208 pp. A woman
finds her Lesbian identity.   ISBN 0-930044-19-3   6.95

PRISM by Valerie Taylor. 158 pp. A love affair between two
women in their sixties.   ISBN 0-930044-18-5   6.95

BLACK LESBIANS: AN ANNOTATED BIBLIOGRAPHY

compiled by J. R. Roberts. Foreword by Barbara Smith. 112 pp.
Award-winning bibliography.   ISBN 0-930044-21-5   5.95

THE MARQUISE AND THE NOVICE by Victoria Ramstetter.
108 pp. A Lesbian Gothic novel.   ISBN 0-930044-16-9   6.95

OUTLANDER by Jane Rule. 207 pp. Short stories and essays
by one of our finest writers.   ISBN 0-930044-17-7   8.95

ALL TRUE LOVERS by Sarah Aldridge. 292 pp. Romantic
novel set in the 1930s and 1940s.   ISBN 0-930044-10-X   7.95

A WOMAN APPEARED TO ME by Renee Vivien. 65 pp. A
classic; translated by Jeannette H. Foster.   ISBN 0-930044-06-1   5.00

CYTHEREA'S BREATH by Sarah Aldridge. 240 pp. Romantic
novel about women's entrance into medicine.
                                           ISBN 0-930044-02-9   6.95

TOTTIE by Sarah Aldridge. 181 pp. Lesbian romance in the
turmoil of the sixties.   ISBN 0-930044-01-0   6.95

THE LATECOMER by Sarah Aldridge. 107 pp. A delicate love
story.   ISBN 0-930044-00-2   6.95

ODD GIRL OUT by Ann Bannon.   ISBN 0-930044-83-5   5.95

I AM A WOMAN by Ann Bannon.   ISBN 0-930044-84-3   5.95

WOMEN IN THE SHADOWS by Ann Bannon.
                                           ISBN 0-930044-85-1   5.95

JOURNEY TO A WOMAN by Ann Bannon.
                                           ISBN 0-930044-86-X   5.95

BEEBO BRINKER by Ann Bannon.   ISBN 0-930044-87-8   5.95
        Legendary novels written in the fifties and sixties,
              set in the gay mecca of Greenwich Village.

VOLUTE BOOKS

JOURNEY TO FULFILLMENT   Early classics by Valerie   3.95

A WORLD WITHOUT MEN   Taylor: The Erika Frohmann   3.95

RETURN TO LESBOS   series.   3.95

These are just a few of the many Naiad Press titles — we are the oldest and
largest lesbian/feminist publishing company in the world. Please request a
complete catalog. We offer personal service; we encourage and welcome
direct mail orders from individuals who have limited access to bookstores
carrying our publications.